The Complete Ramen Cookbook

Quick and Nutritious Everday Meals and Insights on Japanese Cuisine incl. Must-have Ramen Recipes

1st Edition

Hayashi Tanaka

Copyright © [2019] [Hayashi Tanaka]

All rights reserved

The author of this book owns the exclusive right to its content. Any commercial usage or reproduction requires the clear consent of the author.

ISBN- 9781707817054

Table of Contents

Introduction 7
    History 13
    Dining Etiquette 14
    Kitchen Essentials 16

Recipes 19
    Basics 21
        Japanese-Style Rice 22
        Kombu Dashi 23
        Sushi Rice 24
        Teriyaki Sauce 25
        Tofu 26
        Tempura Batter 27
        Grilled Wagyu Steak 28
        Yakisoba Fried Noodles 29
        Tamagoyaki Japanese Omelette 30
        Miso Soup 31
        Cold Green Tea Soba Noodles 32
        Miso Hoikoro Japanese Pork and Cabbage Stir Fry 33
        Beef Tataki Carpaccio 34
        Teriyaki Salmon 36
        Pickled Vegetables 37
        Soba Noodle Salad 38
        Teriyaki beef skewers 39
        Snow Pea Salad 40
        Toshikoshi Soba 41

    Salmon, ginger and soba noodle stir-fry 42

Ramen 45

    Japanese Ramen Noodle Soup 46

    Simple Homemade Ramen 48

    Quick Ramen Noodle Soup 50

    Ramen Noodle and Beef Soup 51

    Vegan Ramen Noodle Soup 53

    Easy Vegan Ramen 55

    Easy Homemade Chicken Ramen 57

    Slow Cooker Beef Ramen 59

    Ramen Chicken Noodle Soup 61

    Vegetarian Ramen with Savoury Broth 62

Japanese Noodles 65

    Yakisoba (Japanese Stir fry noodles) 66

    Japanese Pan Noodles 67

    Hibachi Noodles 68

    Sesame Soba Noodles 69

    Vegetarian Japanese Pan Noodles 70

    Sweet/savoury Japanese Noodles 72

    Chicken Yakisoba 74

Snacks and Desserts 77

    Strawberry Awayukikan Dessert 78

    Japanese Kuri Youkan Chestnut Jelly Cake 79

    Strawberry Daifuku & Matcha Ganache Filling 80

    Onigiri 82

    Japanese Sweet Potato Chips 83

    Teriyaki Chicken & Avocado Wontons 84

Quick 'n Easy Good-for-you Meals 85

    Easy Fried Rice 基本のチャーハン 86

Oyakodon 親子丼 88
Salmon in Foil 鮭のホイル焼き 90
Yasai Itame 野菜炒め 92
Yaki Udon 焼きうどん 94
Baked Tonkatsu 揚げないとんかつ 96
Honey Soy Chicken はちみつ醤油チキン 98
Gyudon 牛丼 99

Must Try Meals 101

Yakisoba Sauce 102
Prawn Gyoza 103
Deep Fried Sushi Rolls 104
Easy Wafu Pasta with Shrimp & Asparagus 海老とアスパラガスの簡単和風パスタ . 106

Disclaimer 108

Introduction

Excerpt from Rice, Noodle, Fish: Deep Travels Through Japan's Food Culture
"What to eat? You've crossed a dozen time zones to get here and you want to make every meal count. Do you start at an izakaya, a Japanese pub, and eat raw fish and grilled chicken parts and fried tofu, all washed down with a river of cold sake? Do you seek out the familiar nourishment of noodles- ramen, udon, soba- and let the warmth and beauty of this cuisine slip gloriously past your lips? Or maybe you wade into the vast unknown, throw yourself entirely into the world of unfamiliar flavours: a bowl of salt-roasted eel, a mound of sticky fermented soybeans, a nine-course kaiseki feast."

— Matt Goulding

There's no need to cross a dozen time zones to enjoy authentic Japanese cuisine; read on to equip yourself to whip up a culinary delight without leaving home.

Cuisine of water is a very apt description of Japanese food, given that the country is entirely surrounded by ocean. The archipelago comprises no less than 3000 islands! A circulatory system of rivers, streams and tumbling waterfalls make up the arteries and veins of the country's life-blood. Considering all this, it makes sense that fish is of such significance in regional and local diets.

To understand the art of Japanese cooking better, the relevance of the number five must be understood. This *Power of Five* is intrinsically threaded through the culture, bleeding inevitably into the national food. Food should be enjoyed through all five senses: taste, sight, hearing, smell, and touch. Kaiseki (懐石) cuisine is a traditional multi-course Japanese dinner and tantamount to Western haute cuisine, which uses this collection of skills and techniques in the preparation of meals. Chef Yoshiyuki best explains: "Kaiseki cuisine is considered to be Japan's top fine dining cuisine because of its beauty, intricacy and the amount of thought and effort put in - from conceptualizing to cooking the dish."

Since time immemorial, Japanese cuisine has been served in small portions, using one of five standard cooking techniques: raw, simmered, steamed, fried, and roasted or grilled.

Foods are divided into *five colour groups*: green, red, yellow, white, and black-purple. Being mindful of this practice, which also has its roots in Buddhism, supports balanced meals incorporating the necessary vitamins and minerals.

Five flavours cater to the sense of taste. Salty, sour, bitter, sweet, and *umami*. Umami originates from *umai* which means delicious and can best be described as savoury.

Less appreciated in the daily preparation and partaking of meals would be the *five attitudes*. The Buddhist faith is once again responsible for the cultivation of this spirit of gratitude:

I contemplate on the work that has resulted in this food; allow me to see where this food is from

I contemplate my imperfections and my deserving this food on offer; Allow me to free my mind of greed and preferences.

I resolve to use this food as a valuable medicine to keep my body healthy.

I accept this food as means to fulfil my enlightenment.

The principal virtues of Japanese cuisine are freshness, seasonality, and simplicity. *Freshness*: fish and meat and the importance placed on its freshness must be appreciated.

Seasonality: Economically and environmentally, selecting fruit and vegetables that are in season just makes sense. They also just taste better!

Simplicity: although the preparation may be elaborate at times, dishes remain essentially aesthetically simple. Fresh produce is washed in water before lightly cooking in water to encourage the natural flavours. Tradition requires dishes of different flavours never touching, which necessitates the serving of dishes partitioned by leaves, or served on separate plates.

With a little practice, and always bearing these three elements in mind, anyone can confidently manage what may be regarded as the art of Japanese food preparation.

Three meals a day are the norm in Japan, as is afternoon and late-night snacking. A meal includes rice, *soup, pickles, and* a minimum of one *side dish*. Dining at home sees these not as separate courses, but rather served together.

Rice, known as *meshi and gohan* 飯, can be regarded as a national staple if not core ingredient in Japan, with a preference for the short-grained variety, traditionally boiled or steamed. In fact, meshi and gohan refer also to a „meal." Rice was however not only for eating but was used in paper and wine production too.

Soup, or *dashi* 出汁, だし, is made up of three basic ingredients in their underlying stock:

- Katsuobushi, or dried bonito,
- Konbu, or kelp, and
- Shiitake mushrooms

The two main soups based on these stocks are:

- Suimono, or clear soups, which are light and elegant, with salt and soy sauce and two or three solid food additives, usually fish, vegetable, or aromatic garnishing.
- Miso soups are made of a paste of soybeans and barley cured for a year or so while infused with a fungal culture. They can be chunky or smooth, sweet or salty, and vary from white to almost black in colour.

Miso soup is most common, high in protein, and very satisfying.

Tsukemono, or *Japanese pickles* are usually made of vegetables, typically cucumbers, eggplants, Daikon radishes, Chinese cabbages, and turnips. Only one fruit is pickled to make *umeboshi*, and that is *ume*, the unripened Japanese plum.

Okazu, or *side dishes*, are prevalent as accompaniment to the basic rice dishes. More extravagant meals may see many side dishes, while a simpler meal will include only one. Okazu include salads, seafood, tofu, and meat:

- *Salads* are served cold and there are two categories: *sunomono*, or vinegared; and *aemono*, with heavier salad dressings.
- *Seafood* is plentiful in a country with so much water. Fresh fish is preferred raw, while less fresh fish is grilled, and less still is stewed with miso or soy sauce. Seafood includes fish, shellfish, and kelp, served as:
  - Sashimi
  - Sushi
  - Wakame
  - Agar-agar (kanten)
  - Nori, the black paper like sheets used to wrap certain sushi
- *Tofu* was introduced in the first century AD by Buddhist priests who were denied meat and fish, as a protein source and is served in a variety of ways as:
  - *Hiyayakko*, bite sized chilled pieces served with grated ginger and a dipping sauce of soy sauce.
  - *Yudoofu*, cubes heated in kelp-seasoned hot water and dipped in a hot sauce flavoured with grated Daikon radish.
  - *Iridoofu* comprises tofu stirred over heat together with shiitake mushrooms, carrots, and snow peas.

▷ Dengaku is skewered tofu roasted and then spread with miso before roasted again.
- *Meat* was more or less a taboo through the ages for cultural and religious reasons. Beef did however become somewhat of a fad in the early 1870s, later endorsed by the emperor in 1873 as customary. The 1930s saw pork become popular. Popular dishes include:

  ▷ Sukiyaki

  ▷ Shabu Shabu

  ▷ Tonkatsu

With beef as a taboo on the table for some thousand years, the Meiji Period between 1868 and 1912 saw it become a delicacy. Indeed, in the 21st century Japanese beef bred in a certain human manner is verily sought after. Wagyu is therefore well worth further explanation. Wagyu is a Japanese word made up of Wa, which means Japanese, and Gyu, which means beef. Japanese Black, Japanese Brown, Japanese Shorthorn and Japanese Polled, the Aberdeen Angus cross, are bred for beef production in Japan. Contemporary Wagyu comes from local breeds crossed with imported beef cattle including Simmental, Brown Swiss, Shorthorn, Ayrshire, Devon, and Korean. In order to qualify as Wagyu, the cattle must be reared and fed in accordance with very stringent guidelines. Calves are hand-reared on specific food that ensures the meat is marbled. They wear jackets to stave off the cold and are sold off to fattening farms at seven months. Calves are raised in barns at these fattening farms, where they are known by name rather than numbered. Each wagyu-quality animal has a birth certificate which means its lineage can be traced. While typical beef is slaughtered at 15 months, these cattle remain on a very specific diet up to a weight of 1550lbs (700kg), typically to 3 years of age. During their growth, antibiotics and added growth hormones are absolutely prohibited. In addition, Wagyu extends to Kobe beef, a highly regarded meat from the Tajima breed, bred exclusively in Japan's Hyogo province. The nitty gritty of wagyu is however the taste. It boasts the highest marbling and finest colour of fat and muscle. The result is such that the fat quite literally melts in your mouth, with a juicy, buttery flavour that is beyond tender, almost silky in texture.

歴史

History

Japanese food is as old as the hills. Over so many centuries it has been unavoidably influenced by the different customs of many countries.

Going back as far as 300BC, we have the Koreans and the Chinese introducing rice to Japan. Japan enthustiastically cultivated rice locally and the rest is very much history. China is also responsible for the Japanese embracing chopsticks, soy sauce, wheat, soybeans, and tofu as their own.

The centuries roll on to 700AD when Buddhism's influence became noteworthy. Meat became taboo in line with the pollo-pescatarian culture of the religion which saw a preference for consuming fish. The Buddha allowed his monks chicken, pork, and fish, provided the monks knew for certain that the 'food' did not die for the purpose of feeding them. This ban on meat led to the popularity of *sushi* in Japan. But what exactly is sushi? Quite simply, raw fish and rice… which was probably also brought across from Korea along with the rice.

Trade between outside countries started around the 13th century, resulting in some Western influences.. Potatoes, sweet potatoes, and corn were brought by the Dutch, and batter frying or tempura originated in Portugal.

行儀

Dining Etiquette

'When in Rome', the saying goes. When eating Japanese as authentically as possible, using *ohashi* or chopsticks is kind of a given. Japanese do eat soup with chopsticks, too. This is done by holding the bowl close to the lips, and sipping. Novice chopstick diners may need a few tips:

- Hold the chopsticks between the right thumb and forefinger. The lower chopstick is held between the tip of the middle and ring fingers and the upper chopstick between index and middle finger. The thumb holds the two chopsticks in place. Only the upper chopstick should move to grasp the food, using thumb, forefinger and middle finger.

- Keep the left hand beneath the food in case of spillage.

- When encountering a piece of food that is too large to eat, simply bite off a managable bite, but never attempt to cut it with the chopsticks.

Definite no-no's when eating with chopsticks:

Tataki-bashi involves using chopsticks to drum on the table or plates

Yose-bashi is the act of using chopsticks to move dishes

Sashi-bashi, pointing at a person or stabbing at the food with chopsticks

Mayoi-bashi, indecisively waving chopsticks over selection of dishes

Koji-bashi, picking from the bottom of a dish rather than from the top

Utsuri-bashi entails lifting food with chopsticks and then deciding rather on something else after a change of mind

Saguri-bashi is the act of seeking out preferred titbits by stirring through the soup

Namida-bashi is the dipping of liquid chopsticks on route to the mouth.

厨房

Kitchen Essentials

There really is no substitute for the right tools for the job to make life just that little bit easier. This rings especially true for preparing Japanese cuisine. While one could make do with alternatives, life is just simpler and meals that much more genuine with certain authentic Japanese cooking equipment.

Suihanki - Automatic Rice Cooker

An absolute blessing for the Japanese food enthusiast. Cook perfect Japanese rice every time.

Shamoji - Rice Paddle

Useful for mixing or scooping rice, the slightly curved paddle is particularly handy.

Hangiri or Ohitsu

Bamboo baskets prove themselves invaluable when mixing and cooling sushi rice. Fluff the cooked rice with a rice paddle before moving it into this wide, flat, breathable container.

Saibashi - Non-lacquered 12 to 17-inch chopsticks

Fill the role of so many gadgets once the techniques have been honed. Frying, turning and simmering food, scrambling eggs, and checking the temperature of oil are just the tip of the iceberg for these useful space savers.

Otoshibuta - Wooden Drop-lid

Very lightweight drop-lid resting on simmering liquid, allowing water to circulate, unlike other lids which have water circulate with it. This allows foods to develop a delightfully light texture.

Makisu - Bamboo Mat

Used for more than just creating the aesthetic appeal of a sushi roll. Press liquid out of tofu and shape Japanese tamagoyaki, rolled omelettes, and French roulades.

Zaru Japanese Bamboo Sieve

To drain, rinse, dry and cool foods, or in which to serve certain dishes.

Oroshigane - Grater Box

With a surface to puree and another to roughly grate, foodstuffs remain on top rather than falling through the grater. Ideal for grating garlic, carrots, daikon radish and horseradish.

製法

RECIPES

Basics

Saying 'Itadakimasu' before eating a meal is to say: "I humbly receive" and serves also as a thank you

They say the best place to start is at the beginning. With Japanese cooking, this would be with the basic recipes, common in many Japanese meals. But also some easy to cook Japanese dishes to dip your toe in while you build your confidence…

Japanese-Style Rice

Time: 60 minutes | Serving: 4

Ingredients:

- 2 ¼ cups short grain rice
- 2¼ cups water

Preparation:

1. Wash rice in cold water until water washes clear. Drain and set aside for 30 mins

2. Stove top method: allow rice to soak in water in pot for 1 hour. Cover and bring to boil over high heat. Reduce to medium heat and simmer for 20 mins. Turn off heat, keep covered and steam for 15 mins. Remove lid, fluff rice with rice spatula and serve

3. Rice Cooker Method: Start the cooker once the rice has soaked for the hour. Turn off and steam for 15 mins. Remove lid, fluff rice with rice spatula and serve.

Kombu Dashi

Time: 37 minutes | Amount: 4 cups

Ingredients:

- 4 cups water
- 8-inch (2½cm) kombu or dried kelp, halved

Preparation:

1. Clean kombu by wiping with clean cloth. Add the kombu to the water in a deep pot, and soak for 30 mins

2. Heat over low heat and remove kombe just before water comes to the boil. Reserve kombu for future use

3. Remove broth and use immediately or refrigerate. Use dashi as basis for miso soup or noodle soup.

Sushi Rice

Time: 90 minutes | Serving: 4 - 6

Ingredients:

- 3 cups Japanese rice
- 3 ¼ cup water
- 2.8 Fl-oz (80ml) rice vinegar
- 3 tbsp sugar
- tsp salt
- Optional: ¼ cup sake-mash OR white-wine vinegar

Preparation:

1. Wash rice in cold water until water washes clear. Drain and set aside for 30 mins

2. Rice Cooker Method: Cook rice in cooker after rice has soaked for 30 mins. Turn off and steam for 15 mins

3. In saucepan, mix rice vinegar, sake-mash vinegar (if desired), sugar, and salt. Heat over low heat to dissolve sugar and then cool

4. Spread cooked rice out on hangiri. Sprinkle rice with vinegar mixture and fold quickly using shamoji, being careful not to mash the rice

5. Tip: waft over sushi with hand-held paper fan to cool, remove moisture and cause a sheen.

Teriyaki Sauce

Time: 15 minutes | Serving: 2 - 4

Ingredients:

- ½ cup soy sauce
- ½ cup mirin
- 2 tbsp sugar
- Optional: 1 tsp garlic/ginger root (chopped)

Preparation:

1. Combine soy sauce, mirin, and sugar in small saucepan, adjusting sugar to taste
2. Add optional garlic and/or ginger if desired
3. Stir while heating over medium-high. Bring to boil, simmer at reduced heat until slightly reduced
4. Remove from heat. Cool. Strain ginger and/or garlic if added.

Tofu

Time: 10 minutes | Serve:

Ingredients:

- 10½-oz (300g) block soft tofu, quartered
- 1 sheet yakinori
- <u>Sauce:</u>
- 2 tbsp Tamari
- 2 tbsp mirin
- ½ tsp dashi stock dissolved in 2 tbsp water

<u>Garnish:</u>

- 1 or 2 spring onions, finely sliced
- 1-2 tbsp finely shaved bonito flakes

Preparation:

1. Line small pan with sheet of yakinori seaweed and top with tofu. Cover tofu with water. Simmer for 6 to 8 mins over low to medium heat. Do not boil!

2. Meanwhile stir together tamari, dissolved dashi stock, and mirin

3. Remove cooked tofu to small serving bowls using slotted spoon/spatula. Serve garnished with spring onions and katsuobushi, with blended tamari sauce over the top.

Tempura Batter

Time: 15 minutes | Amount: 2 cups

Ingredients:

- 1 cup flour, sifted
- 1 egg
- 1 cup ice cold water
- Ice cubes

Preparation:

1. Beat egg gently to just mix yolk and white
2. Combine water and ice cubes, strain out a cup of ice-cold water ensuring no ice is included and add to egg
3. Mix in the sifted flour, using chop sticks and being careful not to over mix
4. Use immediately although it may be refrigerated for only a few minutes until needed.

Grilled Wagyu Steak

Time: 5 minutes | Serving: 1 - 2

Ingredients:

- 12 (340g) oz Japanese Wagyu Steak
- Salt & black pepper

Preparation:

1. Allow steak to come to room temperature and slice into 4 equal portions
2. Heat heavy based cast-iron skillet over very high heat
3. Sear the meat in very hot skillet for 1 min on each side
4. Plate the meat. Rest dish for a minute or two before serving.

Yakisoba Fried Noodles

Time: 8 minutes | Serves: 1

Ingredients:

- 1 portion yakisoba noodles
- 1 tbsp yakisoba sauce
- 1 tbsp mayonnaise
- 0.11lbs (50g) pork, sliced small
- 1 carrot, thinly sliced
- ¼ green pepper, sliced thinly
- ⅛ cabbage, roughly chopped
- ½ onion, roughly chopped
- pickled shredded ginger
- aonori powdered seaweed
- optional: katsuobushi

Preparation:

1. Brown the pork by stir frying it. Add all vegetables except cabbage. Cook until soft, then add cabbage
2. To serve, sprinkle top with aonori and pickled ginger. If desired, katsuobushi and mayonnaise can be added.

Tamagoyaki Japanese Omelette

Time: 10 minutes | Serve: 1

Ingredients:

- 4 eggs, beaten well
- 1 tbsp mirin
- 1 tbsp soy sauce
- cooking oil
- pinch of salt
- 1 tbsp sugar

Preparation:

1. Mix soy sauce, mirin, sugar and salt to beaten egg

2. A dd a little egg mix to heated oil in a pan. Cook lightly, leaving the top slightly uncooked. Put one side

3. Clear pan with kitchen paper towel. Repeat steps 1 & 2. Roll the 1st cooked egg mix over the second mix in pan. Continue step 3, adding new layers until all the egg is used.

4. Remove, cool and slice.

Miso Soup

Time: 5 minutes | Serve: 4

Ingredients:

- 12 oz (340g) tofu, drained
- 6 scallions, thinly sliced
- 4 cups (1 quart) dashi/kombu broth
- ½ cup shiitake mushrooms, soaked & chopped
- 6 tbsp red miso paste

Preparation:

1. Cube tofu. Slice scallions thinly. Set aside
2. Bring the dashi/broth to a simmer over medium high heat
3. In measuring cup, add ½ cup of dashi/broth to miso. Whisk to dissolve miso in liquid, removing lumps
4. Add miso to simmering broth. Reduce heat and add tofu and mushrooms. Simmer to warm tofu, 1 or 2 min. Do not boil
5. Serve sprinkled with scallions.

Cold Green Tea Soba Noodles

Time: 15 minutes | Serve: 2

Ingredients:

- 6½ to 7oz (180-200g) green tea soba noodles
- 1.75oz (50ml) tsuyu dipping sauce
- 2 thinly chopped onions
- wasabi paste
- tempura flakes
- shredded nori seaweed

Preparation:

1. Add soba noodles to 3½ pints (2 litre) boiling water. Boil for 4 or 5 mins. Strain, wash under cold water, and let dry for 5 min

2. Serve sprinkled with shredded nori and tempura flakes on zaru soba tray, with side dishes of tsuyu, green onions, and wasabi.

Miso Hoikoro Japanese Pork and Cabbage Stir Fry

Time: 6 minutes | Serve: 1 - 2

Ingredients:

- 5.6oz (160g) pork belly, sliced into 1-inch (3cm) strips
- ½ clove garlic, minced
- 7oz (200g) cabbage, roughly chopped
- 1 green bell pepper, sliced
- ½ tsp broad bean chilli paste
- 2 tbsp liquid miso with dashi

Preparation:

1. Brown garlic over medium heat in frying pan with 1 tbsp veg oil. Add pork and chilli paste and stir-fry until browned

2. Combine cabbage and green pepper to browned pork and stir-fry until slightly tender, 2 or 3 min. Add liquid miso and stir-fry to reduce liquid. Serve warm.

Beef Tataki Carpaccio

Time: 20 minutes | Serve: 2

Ingredients:

- 10½-oz (300g) beef loin, at room temp
- 2 tbsp sake
- 3-4 tbsp soy sauce
- 2 tbsp mirin
- Optional: 1 tbsp sugar

Toppings

- ½ onion
- lettuce
- tomatoes
- spring onion
- shiso perilla leaves
- watercress
- ponzu

Preparation:

1. Lightly brush oil over beef, season and brown both sides evenly

2. Remove excess oi+l, and add mirin, sake, and sugar as per individual choice. Cook lightly, add soy sauce, cook for 3 to 5 mins, occasionally stirring. Cool in resealable bag in fridge

3. Serve sliced with selected vegetables topped with sauce.

Teriyaki Salmon

Time: 45 minutes | Serve: 4

Ingredients:

- ¼ cup tamari
- 1 tbsp caster sugar
- 2 tbsp mirin
- 4 skinless salmon fillets
- 1 tbsp sake/shaohsing
- Steamed rice, to serve
- 1 tsp sesame seeds

Preparation:

1. Dissolve sugar in tamari, mirin and sake until dissolved. Use this to marinade refrigerated fish for 30 mins

2. Preheat oven 356°F (180°C). Line tray. Place salmon on parchment lined tray and pour over marinade. Bake for 8 to 10 mins

3. Serve with rice, pickled vegetables (recipe below), and sprinkled with sesame seeds.

Pickled Vegetables

Time: 20 minutes | Serve: 4

Ingredients:

- 1 cucumber, halved, seeded, sliced
- 3½-oz (100ml) rice vinegar
- 1 tsp caster sugar
- 1 carrot, cut into thin matchsticks
- ½ daikon radish, cut into matchsticks
- 1 tbsp Japanese pickled ginger, shredded

Preparation:

1. In colander over sink, sprinkle with 2 tsps. salt. Stand for 10 min. Rinse well, then pat dry with paper towel
2. Simmer vinegar and sugar over low heat for 5 mins. Cool slightly, toss with cucumber, carrot, daikon and ginger
3. Chill and serve with the likes of salmon.

Soba Noodle Salad

Time: 15 minutes | Serve: 4

Ingredients:

- 7 oz (200g) dried soba noodles
- 2 scallions/green onion, sliced
- 0.7 oz (20 g) cilantro, chopped
- 1 tbsp white sesame seeds, roasted/toasted

Dressing

- 1 tbsp vegetable oil
- ½ tsp red pepper flakes
- 3 tbsp sesame oil (roasted)
- 3 tbsp honey
- 3⅛ tbsp soy sauce

Preparation:

1. Infuse ½ tsp crushed red peppers in sesame and vegetable oil over medium heat for 3 min in small pan. Cool. Add soy sauce and honey to cooled oil mixture, whisk together until honey is dissolved
2. Cook soba noodles according to package directions. Drain in colander, rinse under cold water to remove starch and add to large bowl
3. Toss soba noodles, dressing, green onion, cilantro, and sesame seeds together
4. Serve chilled.

Teriyaki beef skewers

Time: 30 minutes | Serve: 4

Ingredients:

- 23oz (650g) rump steak, thinly sliced
- ⅓ cup (80ml) teriyaki sauce

Preparation:

1. Thread beef slices folded in half on 8 skewers. Marinate in shallow bowl of teriyaki sauce for 5 mins

2. Heat a chargrill pan over medium-high heat. Remove skewers from marinade and char, 2 mins on each side, cooking through. Serve with Snow Pea salad (recipe below) and rice.

Snow Pea Salad

Time: 5 minutes | Amount: 1 cocktail

Ingredients:

- 8.8 oz (250g) snow peas, halved lengthways
- 1 cucumber, thinly sliced
- 1.7-oz (50g) mixed baby salad leaves
- 2 cups (400g) jasmine rice, cooked

Dressing:

- 1 tsp sesame oil
- 1 tbsp mirin
- 1 tbsp rice vinegar
- 1 tbsp light soy sauce
- 1-2 tsps. wasabi paste
- 1 tsp caster sugar

Preparation:

Boil peas for 1 min in lightly salted water. Drain, rinse and serve with cucumber and salad leaves. Whisk dressing ingredients together. Toss salad to serve.

Toshikoshi Soba

Time: 15 minutes | Serve: 4

Ingredients:

<u>Noodle soup:</u>

- 3 pints (1.5 litre) bonito/kombu kelp dashi stock
- 7 oz (200ml) soy sauce
- 3 ½-oz (100ml) mirin
- 1 tbsp sugar
- Optional: 10½ oz (300ml) tsuyu

<u>Noodles</u>:

- 7 oz (200g) soba noodles
- 3 ½-oz (100g) spring onions, sliced
- 0.7 oz (20g) tempura flakes
- Optional: 5½-oz (150g) kamaboko fish cake

Preparation:

1. Prepare dashi stock in large pan. Add mirin and simmer gently. Add sugar and allow to dissolve before adding the soy sauce
2. Boil 0.9-quart (1 litre) water and add the soba, cooking according to instructions on the packaging. Drain and rinse
3. Re-heat stock and pour into bowls, add noodles. Serve garnished with spring onions and tempura flakes.

Salmon, ginger and soba noodle stir-fry

Time: 30 minutes | Serve: 4

Ingredients:

- 1 tbsp grated ginger
- ¼ cup (60ml) tamari
- 1 tbsp sesame oil
- ¼ cup (60ml) Shaohsing
- 2 bunches broccolini, half stalks lengthways
- 21 oz (600g) salmon fillets, skinless, in 1-inch (3cm) pieces
- ½ bunch spring onions, sliced at angle
- 2 tbsp sunflower oil
- 1 cup (120g) frozen edamame
- 9½-oz (270g) soba noodles, cooked to packet directions, drained
- 2 tsps. sesame seeds

Preparation:

1. To make marinade, combine sesame oil, ginger and 2 tbs tamari, add salmon and marinate for 10 mins

2. Heat 2 tsp oil over high heat in wok and cook half the salmon for 2 or 3 min. Remove and repeat with 2 tsp oil and other half of salmon. Cover with foil. Rest for 5 mins

3 Stir fry spring onion 1 tbs oil in wok for 2 min. Add broccolini, rice wine, 1 tbs tamari, edamame and ¼ cup water. Cook for 3 to 4 mins, stirring until liquid has reduced. Add noodles, salmon, and leftover juices and toss together

4 Serve topped with sesame seeds.

Ramen

This Japanese dish can be translated to pulled noodles and constitutes Chinese wheat noodles in a meat/fish-based broth, flavoured with miso or soy sauce, with pork, nori, menma, or scallion toppings.

Japanese Ramen Noodle Soup

Time: 40 minutes | Serve: 4

Ingredients:

- 0.6-quart (700ml) chicken stock
- 3 halved garlic cloves
- 4tbsp soy sauce, plus extra to season
- 1-inch (3 - 4cm) ginger pieces, sliced
- 1 tsp Worcestershire sauce
- ½ tsp Chinese five spice
- chilli powder
- optional: 1 tsp white sugar
- 0.8lbs (375g) ramen noodles, cooked
- 0.9lbs (400g) cooked chicken breast/pork, sliced
- 2 tsp sesame oil

<u>*Garnish:*</u>

- 4 tbsp sweetcorn
- 3½- oz (100g) baby spinach
- 4 peeled boiled eggs, halved
- sesame seeds
- finely shredded sheet of dried nori,
- green spring onions/shallots, sliced

Preparation:

1. Mix chicken stock, soy sauce, garlic, ginger, , chilli powder, Chinese five spice, Worcestershire sauce and 10½-oz (300ml) water. Boil in large saucepan and simmer for 5 min. Add soy sauce to sweeten or make saltier as desired

2. Fry cooked pork/chicken in sesame oil until slightly brown. Set aside. Divide noodles into four bowls and garnish each with spinach, meat, sweetcorn and 2 egg halves

3. Strain stock and bring back to boil. Divide between the bowls. Add sliced spring onions/shallots, sesame seeds on nori sheet.

Simple Homemade Ramen

Time: 30 minutes | Serve: 4

Ingredients:

- 2 eggs
- 4 minced cloves garlic
- 1 tbsp olive oil
- 4 cups chicken broth
- 1 tbsp ginger, grated
- 4 oz shiitake mushrooms
- 3 x 5.6-ounce (160g) packages refrigerated Yaki-Soba
- 1 tbsp soy sauce
- 3 cups baby spinach
- Optional: 8 slices Narutomaki
- 1 grated carrot
- 2 tbsp chives, chopped

Preparation:

1. Cover eggs in large saucepan with 1 inch (3cm) of water. Boil for 1 minute. Cover and put one side for 8 to 10 mins. Drain well, cool, peel and cut eggs in half

2. Heat olive oil, add garlic and ginger and cook for 1 or 2 mins, stirring frequently until aromatic. Whisk in mushrooms, soy sauce, broth, and 3 cups water

3 Bring to boil. Simmer at reduced heat until mushrooms soften. 10 mins. Add Yaki-Soba, stir, and cook until loosened, 2 or 3 mins. Add Narutomaki, spinach, chives and carrot. Cook for 2 min and serve topped with eggs.

Quick Ramen Noodle Soup

Time: 15 minutes | Serve: 4

Ingredients:

- 1 tbsp oil
- ½ tsp ginger, grated
- 4 sliced scallions
- 1 tbsp minced garlic
- ½ tsp chili sauce/sriracha
- 3 cups beef broth
- 3 cups chicken stock
- 1 tbsp fish sauce
- 1 tbsp soy sauce
- 1 cup water
- Optional: 4 eggs
- 12 oz (340g) package ramen noodles

Preparation:

1. Cook oil, ginger, garlic, scallions, and chili sauce for 2 to 3 mins over medium-high heat, or until aromatic and the scallions soften. Add chicken stock, beef stock, soy sauce, and fish sauce and bring to boil over high heat. Adjust taste if desired. If too salty, compensate with one cup water. Add noodles and eggs and cook according to package instructions
2. Serve.

Ramen Noodle and Beef Soup

Time: 20 minutes | Serve: 4

Ingredients:

- 4 chopped onions
- 1 tbsp finely chopped ginger
- 2 finely chopped cloves garlic
- ¼ tsp red pepper flakes
- 2 cups water
- 4 cups beef broth
- 3 tbsp olive oil
- 1 sweet potato, peeled and diced
- 1 tbsp soy sauce
- 1 tbsp fish sauce
- 8 oz (225g) ramen-style noodles
- 9 oz (250g) sirloin steak
- Bean sprouts
- Chopped fresh cilantro
- Lime wedges

Preparation:

1. Soften onions, ginger, garlic, and red pepper flakes over medium heat in 2 tbsp oil. Add broth, water, sweet potato, fish sauce and soy sauce, and bring to boil. Simmer until the sweet potato is cooked and then season. Add noodles. Cook according to package instructions. Add broth, if needed

2. Meanwhile over high heat cook steak in 1 tbsp oil to taste. Season, Rest for 5 mins. Serve sliced.

Vegan Ramen Noodle Soup

Time: 30 minutes | Serve: 4

Ingredients:

Fried tofu and mushrooms:

- ½ block drained firm tofu, thinly sliced
- 1 tbsp vegetable oil
- 1 tbsp soy sauce
- 3½ oz (100g) stemless shiitake mushrooms

Vegan ramen noodle soup:

- 2 minced cloves garlic
- 1 tbsp vegetable oil
- 1-inch (3cm) ginger, minced
- 6 cups veg broth
- 3 big handfuls baby spinach leaves
- 2 x 4oz (112g) dried ramen noodles
- 1 peeled carrot, grated

Garnish (optional):

- sesame seeds
- soy sauce as desired
- Sriracha

Preparation:

1. In a dish or plastic bag pour soy sauce over tofu. Turn to coat evenly. Heat oil over medium heat in large skillet/pan. Add tofu slices to slowly fry to crispy and golden on both sides. Remove pan and set one side

2. Sauté mushrooms in the same skillet/pan to golden. Pour over remaining soy sauce, stir to coat and remove from heat

3. Make soup by heating oil in a soup pot over medium-high heat. Sauté garlic and ginger, stirring until garlic browns. Add vegetable broth. Boil, add noodles and cook until chewy

4. Just before serving, stir the spinach into the soup until it wilts. To serve divide into bowls, top with desired toppings, tofu, mushrooms, and grated carrots.

Easy Vegan Ramen

Time: 3 hours | Serve: 4

Ingredients:

- 1 tbsp grapeseed oil
- 5 chopped cloves garlic
- 3-inch (9cm) ginger, peeled and diced
- 1 chopped onion
- 6 cups vegetable stock
- 2 tbsp tamari/soy sauce
- ½-oz (14g) dehydrated shiitake mushrooms
- 1 tbsp white/yellow miso paste
- 1 tsp sesame oil
- 8 oz (225g) ramen noodles

<u>*optional toppings*</u>

- ½ cup green onion, chopped
- 10 oz (285g) extra-firm tofu
- Miso-glazed carrots
- Miso-glazed baby bok choy

Preparation:

1. Sauté over medium-high heat, the oil, garlic, ginger, and onion, stirring occasionally for between 5 and 8 mins, until onion browns

2. Add 1 cup vegetable broth to deglaze pan by scraping bits using wooden spoon. Stir in remaining 5 cups vegetable broth, tamari/soy sauce, and mushrooms. Simmer over medium heat, reduce to low, cover and simmer between 1 hour and maximum 2 or 3 hrs, stirring occasionally

3. Season broth and add miso paste. Half hour prior to serving, prepare desired toppings

4. To prepare noodles, bring water to boil to cook ramen noodles according to package directions. Drain and set aside

5. Drain broth and retain mushrooms onions and ginger, if desired, for serving. To serve, divide ramen noodles between four serving bowls. Top with broth and desired toppings.

Easy Homemade Chicken Ramen

Time: 1 hour | Serve: 2

Ingredients:

- 2 boneless chicken breasts
- salt & black pepper
- 2 tsp sesame/vegetable oil
- 1 tbsp butter, unsalted
- 3 tsp minced garlic
- 2 tsp minced ginger
- 3 tbsp soy sauce
- 4 cups chicken stock
- 2 tbsp mirin
- 1 oz (30g) dried shitake mushrooms
- 2 eggs
- 2 x 3 oz (80g) packs ramen noodles
- ½ cup sliced scallions
- Optional to serve: fresh jalapeño slices

Preparation:

1. Preheat oven 700°F (375°C). Season chicken. Melt butter over medium heat and add chicken, skin-side down, using ovenproof skillet. Cook to golden brown, 5 to 7 mins. Turn to cook both sides evenly, another 4 to 5 min. Move to oven and roast between 15 and 20 min. Remove, cover chicken with foil on plate

2. Cook garlic and ginger until softened in large pot over medium heat. Add mirin and soy sauce and mix. Cook for 1 min, add stock, cover, and boil. Simmer uncovered for 5 mins and add mushrooms. Simmer gently for 10 mins, and season.

3. Cover eggs in water and bring to boil. Simmer for 7 to 8 mins before cooling and carefully peeling. Halve lengthwise and set one side

4. Meanwhile thinly slice chicken and set one side. Cook ramen noodles in the boiling water remaining after boiling eggs, 2 or 3 mins until soft. To serve, divide noodles between two large bowls, add chicken slices and ramen broth, and top with scallions, jalapeño and boiled egg.

Slow Cooker Beef Ramen

Time: 8 hrs 20 minutes | Serve: 8

Ingredients:

- 2 lbs (900g) stew meat
- 1 small onion, diced
- 2 tbsp canola oil
- 1 tbsp chopped ginger
- 4-6 cloves garlic, minced
- 8 cups beef broth
- 8 oz (225g) sliced mushrooms
- ¼ cup soy sauce
- 1 tbsp fish sauce
- 2 tsps. sesame oil
- 8 oz (225g) snow peas
- 1 tbsp lime juice
- 3-4 green onions, chopped
- 3-4 packages ramen noodles
- Garnish: fresh chopped cilantro, and Chile oil

Preparation:

1. Season meat and sear over medium-high heat in batches until well browned. Transfer to lightly greased slow cooker. In slow cooker, add onion, ginger, garlic, beef broth, mushrooms, soy sauce, fish sauce and sesame oil, cover and cook on low for 8 hrs

2. About 30 minutes before serving, stir in snow peas, onions and lime juice

3. Meanwhile, cook Ramen noodles according to package directions. In individual bowls, ladle soup over cooked noodles in individual bowls. Garnish with chopped cilantro and chile oil, if desired.

Ramen Chicken Noodle Soup

Time: 25 minutes | Serve: 4

Ingredients:

- 3 ½ cups Chicken Broth
- 1 tsp soy sauce
- dash black pepper
- 1 tsp ground ginger
- 1 carrot, sliced diagonally
- 1 stalk celery, sliced diagonally
- ½ red bell pepper, 2-inch (6cm) strips
- 1 clove minced garlic
- 2 onions, diagonally sliced
- 4 oz (112g) crumbled uncooked ramen noodles
- 1 cup cooked chicken breast, shredded boneless, skinless

Preparation:

1. Bring to boil over medium-high heat broth, ginger, soy sauce, black pepper, carrot, celery, red pepper, onions and garlic
2. Stir in noodles and chicken, reduce to medium heat and cook for 10 min.

Vegetarian Ramen with Savoury Broth

Time: 1 hr 10 minutes | Serve: 4

Ingredients:

- 8 cups vegetable broth
- 2 tbsp vegetable oil, divided
- 1 oz (30g) dried shiitakes
- ¼ cup tamari/soy sauce
- 2 garlic cloves, minced
- 1 onion, thinly sliced
- ½-inch (2cm) minced ginger,
- 1 tbsp butter
- 1 tbsp white miso paste
- 1 tbsp mirin
- 10 oz (285g) baby spinach
- 10 oz (285g) shiitake mushrooms, sliced
- 4 eggs
- 4 servings dry ramen noodles
- 2 sliced scallions
- 6-oz (170g) package baked tofu, at room temperature
- Gomasio
- Toasted sesame oil with hot chili

Preparation:

1. Bring to boil dried shiitake and vegetable broth, cover and remove from heat. Allow mushrooms to steep for between 30 minutes and 24 hours. Remove mushrooms, chop, and remove stems. Puree mushrooms and 1 cup broth. Add to pot with tamari

2. Cook sliced onion in vegetable oil in large frying pan for 5 mins over medium-high heat, stirring regularly, until softened and slightly brown. Add ginger and garlic and cook for 2 mins, stirring. Add to the pot

3. Boil large pot of unsalted water, add spinach. Cook for a minute, until wilted, remove and set aside. Simmer eggs in the pot for 7 mins. Remove, cool in iced water and then peel. Re-boil water add noodles and cook as per package directions. Drain and then divide into bowls

4. Meanwhile, add remaining vegetable oil to the frying pan and heat over medium-high heat. Add sliced shiitakes and salt and stir occasionally until cooked smaller and browned, about 10 mins

5. Simmer broth, remove from heat, whisk in butter, mirin and miso paste. Ladle broth over noodles and arrange spinach and shiitake in each bowl. Slice and arrange tofu in each bowl. Serve with egg halves and garnishing.

Japanese Noodles

Yakisoba (Japanese Stir fry noodles)

Time: 30 minutes | Serve: 3

Ingredients:

- ½ onion
- 1 carrot, julienned
- 3 sliced shiitake mushrooms,
- 4 cabbage leaves, cut small
- 2 onions/scallions diced to 2-inch (6cm)
- ¾ lb (340 g) pork belly/choice of meat/seafood, cut into 1-inches (3cm)
- 2 tbsp vegetable oil
- Freshly ground black pepper
- 16-17oz (450-480g) pack Yakisoba Noodles
- 4-6 tbsp yakisoba sauce (See recipe in this book)

Preparation:

1. Cook meat in wok in oil over medium-high heat. Add carrot and onion and cook for 1 to 2 mins. Add cabbage and cook until tender. Add onion and shiitake and cook for 1 min. Season with pepper

2. Drain yakisoba noodles and rinse in hot water. Separate by hand, add to wok, lowering to medium heat

3. Add Yakisoba Sauce, mix and serve garnished with dried green seaweed and pickled red ginger.

Japanese Pan Noodles

Time: 50 minutes | Serve: 4

Ingredients:

- 10 oz (285g) fresh udon noodles
- ½ tsp sesame oil, divided
- ½ green bell pepper, matchsticked
- 2 carrots,
- 2 cups chopped broccoli
- ½ zucchini, thinly sliced
- 2 tbsp mirin
- 2 tbsp soy sauce
- 3/4 tsp ginger minced
- 1 tbsp chili-garlic sauce

Preparation:

1. Cook udon for 10 to 12 min in pot boiling salted water. Stir occasionally, until noodles are tender but firm. Drain and rinse and stir in sesame oil drops

2. Cook broccoli for 5 mins in heated sesame oil until crunchy. Add carrots and bell pepper, stir for 2 mins, until slightly soft. Add zucchini, cook for 2 mins until slightly softened

3. Stir in mirin, soy sauce, ginger and chili-garlic sauce, and mix in noodles. Stir while cooking for 1 min until sauce is partly absorbed.

Hibachi Noodles

Time: 25 minutes | Serve: 4

Ingredients:

- 1 lb (450g) linguine/noodles, cooked
- 3 tbsp butter
- 3 tbsp sugar
- 1 tbsp teriyaki sauce
- 1 tbsp garlic, minced
- 4 tbsp soy sauce
- 1 tbsp sesame oil
- 1 tbsp sesame seeds
- Salt and pepper

Preparation:

1. Sauté garlic in butter in a wok over medium-high heat until aromatic. Mix in the noodles and add sugar, soy sauce, teriyaki sauce. Season with salt pepper
2. Remove from heat and drizzle in sesame oil
3. Serve hot, sprinkled with sesame seeds.

Sesame Soba Noodles

Time: 20 minutes | Serve: 6

Ingredients:

- 10 oz (285g) Soba Noodles
- ⅓ cup Soy Sauce
- 3 tbsp toasted sesame oil
- 2 tbsp rice vinegar
- 1 tbsp sugar
- ¼ tsp freshly ground black pepper
- 1 tbsp canola oil
- 2 cups onions chopped in ¼ -inch (6mm) pieces
- ½ cup minced green onions,
- 3 tbsp toasted sesame seeds

Preparation:

1. Cook soba noodles in boiling water until tender, 4 to 5 mins. Stir occasionally stir to prevent clumping. Drain in colander and rinse under cold water

2. Meanwhile, whisk soy sauce, sesame oil, rice vinegar, sugar and black pepper together

3. Cook chopped onions in heated oil over medium-high heat, stirring, between 15 and 30 seconds until aromatic. Add soy and sesame mixture and cook for 30 secs. Add noodles, tossing until heated through. Add half the sesame seeds and remaining onion. Serve garnished with sesame seeds.

Vegetarian Japanese Pan Noodles

Time: 20 minutes | Serve: 4

Ingredients:

- ¼ cup soy sauce
- ¼ cup water
- ¼ cup hoisin sauce
- 1 tsp ginger, minced
- 1-2 tsps. vegetable oil
- 1 cup broccoli florets
- 1 cup shiitake mushrooms, sliced
- ¼ cup shredded carrots
- 9 oz (250g) package udon noodles

Optional topping:

- 1 onion, finely sliced
- ½ cup Asian bean sprouts
- 1 tsp black sesame seeds

Tofu:

- ⅓ block tofu, extra firm
- 1 tbsp corn starch
- 1 tsp vegetable oil

Preparation:

1. Whisk soy sauce, hoisin sauce, water and ginger together. Retain 1 tbs sauce

2. Warm oil in wok for 1-2 mins over high heat and add mushrooms, carrots and broccoli, cooking for 3 mins. Add ⅓ sauce. Cook for 2 mins

3. Add udon noodles and ⅓ of the sauce. Cook while stirring for 5 mins, coating noodles in sauce. Add remaining ⅓ of sauce and remove from heat

4. Meanwhile prepare tofu by drying the cubes using paper towel before tossing in corn starch. Add salt. Heat oil over high heat and add tofu cubes and 1 tbsp sauce. Cook for 1 to 2 mins per side, forming brown crust. Remove from heat, add tofu and combine with noodles in wok

5. Serve in 4 bowls garnished with green onions, bean sprouts, and black sesame seeds.

Sweet/savoury Japanese Noodles

Time: 30 minutes | Serve: 6

Ingredients:

- 2 x 9-oz (225g) packages Japanese-style Noodles, cooked, drained, rinsed
- 1 punnet mushrooms, sliced
- 2 tbsp canola oil
- 5 or 6 chopped cabbage leaves,
- 20-oz (570g) tin pineapple chunks
- 1 pack slightly defrosted frozen brussels sprouts, diced
- 8 scallions, cleaned, trimmed, & chopped (2 for garnish)
- 1 small salami OR 2 to 3 sliced Chorizo sausages

<u>Sauce</u>

- ¼ cup rice vinegar
- 6 tbsp soy sauce
- ⅔ cup brown sugar
- ½ cup honey
- 4 tbsp chili sauce
- 2 cubes Frozen Ginger
- 4 cubes Frozen Garlic
- 2 tsp corn-starch, dissolved in water
- black pepper

Preparation:

1. Sauté mushrooms, cabbage and pineapple in oil, until cabbage wilts. Add brussels sprouts - sauté for 1 min and add sauce ingredients. Simmer until thickened

2. Add noodles and salami and coat in the sauce mixture. Stir in scallions and serve garnished with chopped scallions.

Chicken Yakisoba

Time: 30 minutes | Serve: 4

Ingredients:

- 1 tbsp soy sauce
- 1 ½ tsps. Worcestershire sauce
- 1 tbsp mirin
- 1 tsp sugar
- 1 tbsp oyster sauce
- 8 oz (225g) chicken thighs/breast, sliced
- 2 tsps. corn-starch
- 3 tbsp + 2 tsp oil, divided
- 12 oz (340g) yakisoba noodles
- 6 shiitake mushrooms, sliced thinly
- minced
- 1 medium carrot, julienned
- 2 scallions, julienned
- 1 small onion, sliced thinly

Preparation:

1. Mix soy sauce, mirin, oyster sauce, Worcestershire sauce, and sugar
2. Mix chicken with corn starch and 2 tsps. oil in separate bowl and set aside

3 Heat 1 tbsp oil over high heat in wok and sear chicken in single layer for 1 minute. Stir-fry for a minute, remove and set one side

4 Stir fry shiitake mushrooms in 2 tbsp oil in wok. Add carrots, onions, and cabbage and stir-fry for 2 mins before adding seared chicken, noodles, scallions, and sauce mixture. Stir-fry for 2 to 3 mins until noodles are heated through.

Snacks and Desserts

Strawberry Awayukikan Dessert

Time: 10 minutes | Serve: 2 to 3

Ingredients:

- 5 strawberries, washed, stalks removed
- ½-pint (300ml) water
- 1 egg white
- 0.15 oz (4g) powdered kanten agar agar
- 1.8-oz (50g) sugar

Preparation:

1. Slice 2 strawberries thinly and mash remaining strawberries using a fork
2. Mix water with gelatine and bring to boil over medium heat, reducing to low, and stirring to fully dissolve
3. Add sugar and mashed strawberries to the pan. Stir well, turn off heat and cool to room temperature
4. Whisk egg white in separate bowl until stiffened. Slowly add gelatine mixture
5. Arrange strawberries in container lined with parchment paper and pour mix over strawberries. Refrigerate until firm
6. To serve, remove from container and turn over so strawberry slices are visible from the top. Slice into 2 or 3 portions.

Japanese Kuri Youkan Chestnut Jelly Cake

Ingredients:

- Chopped kuri kanroni chestnuts in syrup,
- 1.8 oz (50g) azuki paste
- ⅓-oz (10g) kanten powdered agar
- 7 oz (200g) sugar
- 0.4-quart (470ml) water

Preparation:

1. Stir water and kanten powder over medium heat. Dissolve kanten powder, reduce heat and cook for 5 mins. Add sugar, stir until dissolved and then whisk in chestnuts and azuki paste. Pour into container and refrigerate to cool

2. Refrigerate for at least 2 hours to allow jelly cake to set. Remove from fridge and cut as desired.

Strawberry Daifuku & Matcha Ganache Filling

Serve: 3 to 6

Ingredients:

- 6 strawberries, refrigerated and trimmed
- 3½-oz (100g) shiratamako
- ¼- pint (150ml) water
- ⅔-oz (20g) sugar
- corn flour for dusting
- <u>Matcha ganache:</u>
- 2 tsp matcha powder
- 3 tbsp double cream
- 5⅓-oz (150g) white choc

Preparation:

1. Mix chocolate and double cream over a pan of boiling water. Lower heat substantially and stir chocolate until melted. Remove from heat

2. Mix matcha powder with a little water in small bowl, and stir until thick and dissolved, making sure it is free of lumps. Add matcha mixture to chocolate and mix well. Set aside and cool

3. Use chopsticks to dip strawberries in ganache. Refrigerate to harden slightly

4 Combine shiratamako and sugar, adding a little water at a time, stirring until smooth. Microwave for 1 minute, mix with spoon and microwave for a minute more. Mix again. Microwave one last time for 30 seconds at which time mixture should be thick

5 Divide daifuku mixture on clean surface dusted with cornflour into six equal pieces. Mould each piece into a thin 3 inch (7cm) flat circle. Place a ganache-coated strawberry in the centre of each daifuku round. Stretch daifuku round to cover filled strawberry .Twist the round closed and twist, rolling in your hands to evenly shape.

Onigiri

Ingredients:

- 3 cups cooked Japanese sticky rice
- water
- 1.7oz (50g) packet rice seasoning (furikake)
- salt

Preparation:

1. Thoroughly mix cooked rice and furikake or rice flavouring evenly. Separate into equal portions of a large handful. Wet hands and rub together with a pinch of salt to prevent sticking

2. Pick up a portion of rice. If you are hiding a surprise inside, indent it and put in the ingredient, folding over to make a ball

3. Press into triangular shape as best you are able

4. Place nori slice on bottom of onigiri with rough side facing rice and fold it upwards to the centre. Repeat for all rice portions

Japanese Sweet Potato Chips

Time: 35 minutes | Serve: 4

Ingredients:

- 2 large sweet potatoes (peeled, thinly sliced)
- ½ tsp herbed sea salt
- 1 tsp olive oil
- lemon zest

Preparation:

1. Preheat oven to 415°F (210°C). Line large sheet pan with parchment paper
2. Toss sweet potato slices in olive oil and herbed sea salt to taste
3. Once well combined lay the slices flat on the sheet and bake for 25-30 mins until brown. Before serving, toss with fresh lemon zest, fine sea salt, and wild herbs. Serve with dip of your choosing.

Teriyaki Chicken & Avocado Wontons

Time: 40 minutes | Serve: 4

Ingredients:

- 2 lb (900g) Chicken breast
- 1 cup Teriyaki sauce
- 1 clove garlic
- 1 tsp ginger
- 1 package Wonton wrappers
- 1 egg
- 2 avocados
- Oil as needed

Preparation:

1. Cook chicken breast and teriyaki sauce in a pan with minced garlic and ginger. Meanwhile mash one avocado. Chop cooked chicken into chunks

2. Beat egg and set one side

3. Edge each wonton wrapper with beaten egg, fill with dollop of avocado and a little chicken and close in shape of your choice. Once all the wontons are ready, heat oil and fry. Serve and enjoy!

Quick 'n Easy Good-for-you Meals

Easy Fried Rice 基本のチャーハン

Time: 20 minutes |

Tips

Day-old rice out the fridge is just the ingredient for this meal. It must however be brought to room temperature so that it does not have to spend too long heating in the wok. To make sure your fluffy egg is never over cooked, let the beaten egg cook up in a pool of hot oil first. Try adding the fluffy egg back in the wok once you have cooked your rice and other ingredients. Limit your ingredients to 3 or 4 and keep it simple. Some suggestions are:

BBQ pork; Chicken; Chinese sausage; Crab; Edamame; Eggs; Green peas; Pork minced meat; Ham; Onion; Salmon; Shrimp

Ingredients:

- 2 rice bowls cooked rice already at room temperature
- 2 slices ham cut into ¼ inch (1cm) squares
- 1 green onion/scallion, whites cut into rounds and green cut diagonally
- 1 egg, whisked
- 2 tbsp vegetable oil, divided
- ½ tsp sea salt and white pepper powder
- 2 tsp soy sauce

Preparation:

1. Swirl 1 tbsp oil in heated wok over medium-high heat to evenly coat surface. Add beaten egg, mixing to make it fluffy. Take care not to overcook by removing the egg while some remains a little runny

2. Stir fry ham in 1 tbsp oil with white green onion rounds to coat well with oil. Add cooked rice, separating with a spatula to fluff rice up and coat with oil. Return fluffy egg to wok, breaking into smaller pieces and combining with rice. Season

3. Add soy sauce, tossing and fluffing fried rice. Add green diagonally cut onion and toss a little before removing to plate

4. To serve sprinkle green onion on top.

Oyakodon 親子丼

Time: under 30 minutes |

What came first? The chicken or the egg? With this meal, it doesn't matter. Just enjoy both as a simple, nutritious and easy to prepare meal. This chicken and egg bowl prepared in one pan has chicken, onions, and egg simmered in an umami-rich dashi-based sauce. Enjoyed over a bowl of fluffy rice, it is comfort food at its best, ready in under 30 minutes.

Ingredients:

- 2 chicken thighs, boneless & skinless
- ½ onion, thinly sliced
- 2 eggs

<u>Choose as many seasons as you like of:</u>

- 1½ tbsp mirin
- 2/3 cup dashi
- 1 ½ tbsp soy sauce
- 1 ½ tsp sugar
- 1 ½ tbsp sake

<u>To serve:</u>

- 3 cups cooked rice
- chopped Mitsuba/scallion/green onion
- Shichimi Togarashi for sprinkling

Preparation:

1. Mix together mirin, dashi, sake, and soy sauce. Add sugar and mix until dissolved

2. Diagonally slice chicken thigh into 1½ " (4 cm) pieces. Beat one egg at a time for each batch in a small bowl

3. Divide ingredients into 2 equal batches for cooking. In a frying pan, layer half the onion and pour about ½ the seasonings mixture over

4. Top the onion with half the chicken distributing evenly. Bring to boil over medium heat. Reduce heat to medium-low, remove foam, cover and cook for 5 mins

5. Slowly drizzle beaten egg over chicken-onion mixture, cover and cook over medium-low heat until done. Add mitsuba/green onion and then remove from heat

6. To serve pour mixture over steamed rice drizzled with remaining sauce to taste. Sprinkle Shichimi Togarashi as an option.

Salmon in Foil 鮭のホイル焼き

Time: 20 minutes |

HA-ke no Hoiru Yaki is delicious, fast, and simple and ideal when you are short of time.

Ingredients:

- 2 salmon fillets 8½-oz (240 g)
- salt and freshly ground black pepper
- ½ onion, thinly sliced
- 2-inch (5 cm) carrot, julienned
- 1.8 oz (50 g) shimeji mushrooms
- 2 shiitake mushrooms
- 2 chives, cut into small pieces
- 1 tbsp sake, divided
- 1 ½ tbsp unsalted butter, divided
- 2 tbsp ponzu/soy sauce, for drizzling

Preparation:

1. Prepare 2 x 12" x 12" (30 x 30 cm) aluminium foil sheets and thinly spread butter in the centre of both
2. Sprinkle both sides of salmon with seasoning. Break up shimeji by hand and slice shiitake thinly

3 Arrange half of the onion slices on the foil with salmon on top, skin side down, and top with the mushrooms, carrot julienne, ½ tbsp sake and ½ tbsp butter

4 Fold foil over salmon a few times from bottom and sides making sure its tightly closed without openings. Repeat with the other salmon

5 Put both salmon in foil on frying pan, cover and cook for 2 min over medium heat. Reduce heat and cook for 10 mins. To serve, open the foil, sprinkle with chives and drizzle with ponzu/soy sauce.

Yasai Itame 野菜炒め

Time: 15 minutes

Stir Fry Vegetables. In Japanese, "yasai (野菜)" means vegetables and "itame (炒め)" means stir fry. This dish is complete with thinly sliced pork or sausages for non-vegetarians to enjoy

Ingredients:

- 6½ oz (185g) thinly sliced pork
- 10 snow peas, prepared
- ¼ onion, thinly sliced
- ¼ cabbage cut into 1" (2.5 cm) pieces
- ½ carrot , cut into matchsticks
- 1 clove garlic, crushed
- 1-inch (2.5 cm) ginger, minced
- 1 tbsp vegetable oil
- 2 cups bean sprouts, loosely packed

Pork Marinade

- 1 tsp soy sauce
- 1 tsp sake

Seasonings

- 1 tsp soy sauce
- 1 tsp oyster sauce
- 2 tsp sesame oil, roasted

- ♦ Salt and pepper

Preparation:

1. Marinate bite sized meat in 1 tsp soy sauce and 1 tsp sake

2. Heat 1 tbsp vegetable oil over medium-high heat in wok and add garlic and ginger, cooking until fragrant. Add meat and cook to 80% done. Add onion, stir fry until almost tender, and add carrot. When carrot is tender, add cabbage and snow peas. Stir and toss

3. Add bean sprouts, toss once, and add oyster sauce and soy sauce

4. Season to taste and drizzle with sesame oil before serving.

Yaki Udon 焼きうどん

Time: 25 minutes |

Stir-fried udon noodles with meat and veg can be made with leftovers, as long as you use only the chewy thick white udon noodles. Leave out the meat and it makes a nutritious vegetarian meal, simple and quick to prepare

Ingredients:

- 2 Udon noodles
- ½ onion, sliced
- 2-3 cabbage leaves cut into 1" (2.5 cm) squares
- 1 carrot, julienned
- 2 shiitake mushroom tops, sliced
- 2 green onions/scallions, sliced
- ½ lb (227 g) pork belly/meat/seafood/vegetables cut into 1" (2.5 cm) pieces
- 1 tbsp vegetable oil

Seasonings

- 1 tsp soy sauce
- black pepper
- 3 tbsp mentsuyu

Toppings

- 3 tbsp katsuobushi
- Optional: 1 tbsp pickled red ginger

Preparation:

1. Cook, drain and rinse the noodles

2. Heat oil over medium high heat in pan and cook pork until very nearly cooked through. Add onion, cooking until translucent

3. Stir fry carrots and cabbage and then add scallion and shiitake mushrooms. Stir fry until all lightly wilted

4. Add udon noodles, combining well using tongs. Season with black pepper, Mentsuyu, and soy sauce to taste. To serve, sprinkle with bonito flakes and top with green onions. Garnish with pickled ginger if desired.

Baked Tonkatsu 揚げないとんかつ

Time: 30 minutes | Serve: 2

Tips

Juicy pork chop encased in crispy panko, deep fried to delight the taste buds. To ensure crispy and golden-brown panko, pre-cook panko before you bread the pork. The pork must be at most ½ inch (1.2 cm) thick and of good quality.

Ingredients:

- ½ lb (227g) 2 x ½»-thick (1.2 cm) pork loin chops, boneless
- 1 tbsp extra virgin olive oil
- ¾ cup panko (Japanese breadcrumbs)
- Salt and Pepper
- 2 tbsp flour
- 1 egg
- Tonkatsu Sauce
- 1 tbsp white and black sesame seeds, roasted/toasted

Preparation:

1. Preheat oven to 400°F (200°C) and line baking sheet with parchment paper

2. Toast panko until golden brown in oil over medium heat. Transfer to shallow dish to cool

3. Trim off extra fat and slit between the meat and fat to prevent the meat from curling up during cooking. Pound meat with meat pounder or back of heavy knife. Season

4 Coat pork in flour, and then egg wash in beaten egg before coating with toasted panko, pressing flakes to adhere to the meat

5 Bake pork on prepared baking sheet until cooked through, 20 mins. When cutting Tonkatsu into bite sized pieces, press knife directly down and do not saw back and forth. Serve immediately

6 For special sesame tonkatsu sauce, grind black and white sesame seeds in a mortar and mix into tonkatsu sauce.

Honey Soy Chicken はちみつ醬油チキン

Time: 1 hour | Serve: 3

Ingredients:

- 1.5 lb (680 g) chicken drumettes
- Salt and freshly ground black pepper

Seasoning:

- 4 tbsp honey
- 4 tbsp soy sauce
- 2 tbsp sake

Preparation:

1. Rinse chicken, pat dry, and prick with fork. Season. Combine seasoning in Ziploc bag and add drumettes. Remove all the air and zip the bag. Coat drumettes and marinate for 30 to 60 mins or overnight

2. Preheat oven to 425°F (218°C). Place drumettes skin side up on baking pan and cover with marinade. Bake for 20 to 30 mins, basting two or three times. Brown under grill if not browned satisfactorily

3. Serve immediately.

Gyudon 牛丼

Time: 20 minutes |

Japanese Beef Bowl is a comfort food that is easily prepared in less than a half an hour.

Ingredients:

- 1 onion, sliced
- 2 green onions/scallions, sliced
- 12 oz (340g) thinly sliced beef chuck/rib eye
- 1 tbsp vegetable oil
- Optional: 3 beaten eggs

<u>Sauce</u>

- 2 tsp sugar
- 2 tbsp mirin
- 2 tbsp sake
- 1 tbsp soy sauce

<u>To Serve</u>

- 3 cups cooked rice
- Garnish: pickled red ginger

Preparation:

1. Cook onions until tender in heated oil over medium high heat. Add meat and sugar and cook through. Add mirin, sake, and soy sauce, and reduce heat. Simmer for 2 to 3 mins

2. If opting to add egg, slowly drizzle beaten egg evenly over the beef, and then cover. Cook till egg is done. Add onion just before removing from heat

3. Serve beef and egg on steamed rice with cooking sauce to taste, topped with green onion and pickled red ginger.

Must Try Meals

Yakisoba Sauce

Time: 4 minutes | Amount: ½ cup

Ingredients:

- 2 tsp sugar
- 4 tsp oyster sauce
- 2 tsp soy sauce
- 4 tsp tomato sauce
- 4 tbsp Worcestershire sauce
- Optional toppings
- Aonori
- pickled red ginger

Preparation:

Whisk all ingredients and set aside.

Prawn Gyoza

These pan-fried Japanese dumplings are typically filled with pork and cabbage or Chinese chives. But the options are endless

Ingredients:

- 20 gyoza wrappers
- 5.2 oz (150g) prawns, chopped small
- 1 tbsp soy sauce
- ½ onion, finely chopped
- 1 tsp ginger paste
- salt and pepper
- tbsp corn starch

Preparation:

Combine prawns, soy sauce, seasoning, ginger paste and corn starch. Wrap with gyoza wrappers, fry adding a little water to pan, and covering to steam fry for 2 to 3mins.

Deep Fried Sushi Rolls

Ingredients:

- 2 cups cooked Sushi rice, seasoned
- Fresh/Smoked Salmon
- Cucumber
- Cream Cheese
- 1 Egg
- 1.8oz (50g) Flour
- Salt & Pepper
- Chili Powder
- 3½ - 5½-oz (100-150g) Panko Breadcrumbs
- 1 Fresh Lime
- Japanese Mayonnaise
- 4 Sheets Nori
- 10½-fl. Oz (300ml) Vegetable Oil

Preparation:

1. Add sushi rice to nori sheets on a bamboo rolling mat, to thickness of 0.4" (1cm) allowing 1" (2cm) gap at top to roll. Pat tightly. Arrange salmon lengthwise, cucumber and cream cheese in sushi roll. Roll the sushi roll as tightly as possible, leaving no visible seam of rice

2. Have beaten egg in a large bowl, a plate of seasoned flour, and a plate of panko breadcrumbs set one side. Heat vegetable oil in pan large enough to accommodate your roll

3 Coat each maki roll in flour, egg wash and evenly coat in panko breadcrumbs. Pat down. Fry maki roll in hot oil until the panko is golden.

4 Slice into sushi pieces and serve with Mayo and lime juice dip.

Easy Wafu Pasta with Shrimp & Asparagus
海老とアスパラガスの簡単和風パスタ

Time: 30 minutes | Serve: 2

Wafu (和風) means Japanese-style. This nutritious pasta dish is a Japanese variation of a Western favourite. If asparagus don't excite you, you have options. Try: Artichokes, Cabbage, Collard greens, Fava beans, Fennel, Green beans, Peas, Snow peas, spinach/Swiss chard, or Watercress.

Ingredients:

- 8 oz (225g) pasta
- ¼ red onion, sliced thinly
- 2 cloves garlic, sliced thinly
- 6 oz (170g) asparagus, separate spears & stalks, cut diagonally
- 10 (0.6 oz/260g) large prawns, peeled, deveined
- salt & freshly ground black pepper
- 1 tbsp extra virgin olive oil
- ¼-⅓ cup (60-80 ml) dashi
- 1½-2 tbsp unsalted butter
- 1 tbsp soy sauce

<u>Optional:</u>

- red pepper flakes
- 1-2 dried red chili peppers, seeds removed

Preparation:

1. Cook Pasta in 16 cups of fast boiling clean water to which 2 tbsp salt has been added. Cook for 1 minute less than package directions

2. Season prawns with salt and pepper

3. Brown bottom of prawns in 1 tbsp olive oil over medium heat, 2 to 3 mins. Flip and brown other side. Set one side on plate

4. Reduce to medium low and coat bottom of pan with butter. Sauté garlic and red onion for 1 minute. Add chilli pepper, if desired. Increase heat to medium and sauté asparagus stalks for 3 mins until tender. Sauté asparagus spears for 1 to 2 mins

5. Up heat to medium high and return prawn to skillet, adding soy sauce to taste

6. Toss cooked pasta into prawn mix and season if required

7. To serve garnish with chili pepper flakes if desired.

Disclaimer

The opinions and ideas of the author contained in this publication are designed to educate the reader in an informative and helpful manner. While we accept that the instructions will not suit every reader, it is only to be expected that the recipes might not gel with everyone. Use the book responsibly and at your own risk. This work with all its contents, does not guarantee correctness, completion, quality or correctness of the provided information. Always check with your medical practitioner should you be unsure whether to follow a low carb eating plan. Misinformation or misprints cannot be completely eliminated. Human error is real!

Picture: Elena Eryomenko // www.shutterstock.com

Design: Oliviaprodesign

Printed in Great Britain
by Amazon